THIS JOURNAL BELONGS TO:

CARLY

D1372165

# BE DARING AND FIND YOUR TRUTH

**TRUTH OR DARE** is one of those party games that's equal parts thrilling and stressful. What if you get asked a truth question you don't want to answer? What if the dare is scary? Add in the fact that everyone is watching and listening, and it really plays on fear—fear that you won't say or do the right thing, fear of failure, fear of blurting out what's really on your mind, fear of what you'll find if you look deep inside.

But what would happen if none of those fears was an issue?

Imagine you're playing truth or dare but there's nobody else around, no one to hear your raw, honest answers to personal questions. Nobody to see you work up the courage for a dare. It's just you. You're doing the truth-telling and you're doing the daring.

If you're playing truth or dare on your own, you might still feel fear—the kind of fear that comes when you challenge yourself to do something a little out of your comfort zone, something that will push you or help you take a leap when you would normally hold back—but that's good fear, the kind of fear that stretches us, that makes us human.

It makes perfect sense that the game of truth or dare has become a cultural touchstone, staying popular and relevant for many generations of people. You can only find your truth when you are brave enough to push yourself deeper than the surface. And that takes daring. You can't have one without the other.

My hope is that this journal will challenge you, and help you discover the courage, compassion, and curiosity already in you. When you dig down to reveal what moves you, what brings meaning into your life, it will then spur you to seek new experiences, to try new things and have new adventures.

If you're feeling thoughtful, flip to a Truth page in this book and let your mind—and pen—go wild. If you're feeling bold, let loose and take on a Daring page challenge. No rules, no pressure—this is all about you. You're the one in charge here. And you are so much stronger than you think.

Inside you'll also find blank space for thoughts or activities, as well as inspiring quotes from gutsy women who have paved the way when it comes to living with truth *and* daring. Tear the quotes out and tape them up on your bathroom mirror, next to your bed, or wherever you're most likely to see them as you go about your day. Or write your own. After all, you're gutsy and inspiring, too.

So go on—turn the page, be daring, and find your truth!

XXX Sarah

# TRUTH

When you look in the mirror, what do you see? What's the first thing you think about yourself? when I look in the mirror I See, a true dancer, a Young girl who is strong, a caring girl, a nice little girl, a adventuress girl, a tough girl, a small girl, a cool girl.

# TRUTH & DARING

## A JOURNAL FOR THE THOUGHTFUL & BOLD

By Sarah O'Leary Burningham

Illustrated by Sarah Walsh

chronicle books
san francisco

**For Nora.** May your life be filled with truth *and* daring. —S. B.

**Michele,** you've never been afraid to be yourself.
Keep daring and living your truth. —S. W.

Create a personal mantra, words *you* want to live by. It might be a few words, or it might be a few sentences. It could encapsulate who you are and what you want your life to be. It could be something you can repeat to yourself during moments of self-doubt, when you need a little clarity, or just when you look at yourself in the mirror while you're brushing your teeth. If coming up with a mantra feels daunting, you can borrow mine. I often say to myself, "You are the still center of a spinning wheel." It's a reminder that no matter how much is going on in my life, no matter how many things are "spinning" around me, I am still me. I am constant, and I don't have to be affected by everything. My mantra reassures me.

Come back to this idea of a mantra once you've finished this journal. Has your personal mantra evolved as you've discovered and experienced new things? Give yourself permission to add to it or even rewrite it, and do that as often as you need to! As you grow and change, your mantra is likely to grow and change with you.

**TRUTH**

What is the most meaningful gift you've ever received?

Give something you love—or something you'll miss—to someone else, someone you think will appreciate or benefit from it. It doesn't have to be a special
occasion, and it's even better if it's not. How does it feel to give something
that's important to you to someone else?

# TRUTH

If I could make a living doing anything, I would be . . .

# DARING

Find someone who has your dream job and ask to interview them. If you don't get a response when you first reach out, don't give up. After some time has passed, try following up in a new way, like by sending a card. Or try someone else at the company. Keep trying until you get the conversation you're craving. Make a list of questions to prepare, and stay present during the conversation. Then record what you've discovered. How did they get to where they are now? What advice did they have for you? What are you going to do to pursue your dream?

# TRUTH

Whose love has changed you for the better?

_____

_____

_____

_____

_____

_____

_____

_____

_____

_____

_____

_____

_____

_____

_____

_____

_____

_____

_____

_____

_____

_____

_____

Tell someone you love that you love them. Don't write it down.

SAY IT
OUT
LOUD.

# TRUTH

What is your most important childhood memory?

DARING

Make a good moment last longer. Soak it in. Turn your phone off. Shut your laptop. Breathe through your nose. Smell the air. Close your eyes for a few seconds. What does the moment sound like? Look—really *look*—around. Take it all in. Write down your observations after it's all over. What do you remember? When you need a happy thought, come back to this page and that good moment.

# TRUTH

My relationship with my body is . . .

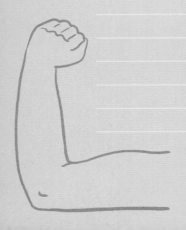

Make a list of all the things your body has done for you today. Now write a thank-you note to your body. Read it out loud.

# THANK YOUR BODY.

# TRUTH

What book has changed your life?

Help that book change someone else's life, too. Write a note about why that book is so important to you. Go to your local library and tuck your note into the book for someone else to find.

"LIFE IS A VERB NOT A NOUN."

—CHARLOTTE PERKINS GILMAN,
feminist, sociologist, and writer

# TRUTH

I am happiest when . . .

# PLAN SOMETHING YOU CAN LOOK FORWARD TO.

Maybe you're going to hang out with a friend. Maybe you're going to start a book you've been dying to read. Maybe you're going to make your favorite tacos for dinner. Having something small in your life to look forward to, something tiny you can celebrate, will make you happier right now, not just in the future.

**TRUTH**

What's the best meal you've ever eaten?

_____
_____
_____
_____
_____
_____
_____
_____
_____
_____
_____
_____
_____
_____
_____
_____
_____
_____
_____
_____
_____
_____
_____
_____
_____
_____
_____

Many famous chefs say that everything tastes better when it's made with love. Today, make something and feel the love while you're making it. Then taste it. Does it taste better than it normally does?

# TRUTH

What do you spend the most time thinking about?

# DARING

Find a place where you won't be disturbed and sit in silence for the next 15 minutes. If the phone rings, don't answer it. If someone texts, don't respond. Try to sit there and listen to the silence. What does it sound like? Where does your mind go? Notice the physical sensations in your body, whatever they may be. How do you feel when the 15 minutes are over?

# DOUBLE DARING

Try this same 15 minutes of silence every day for a week. How does it change from day to day? Are some days harder than others, or does it get easier with time? If after a week you notice that you're better able to deal with stress or have a different sense of calm (or even if you just like having 15 minutes to yourself), consider making this a regular practice.

Do you think you're lucky? Or do you make your own destiny?

Write the fortune you wish you would find in a fortune cookie.

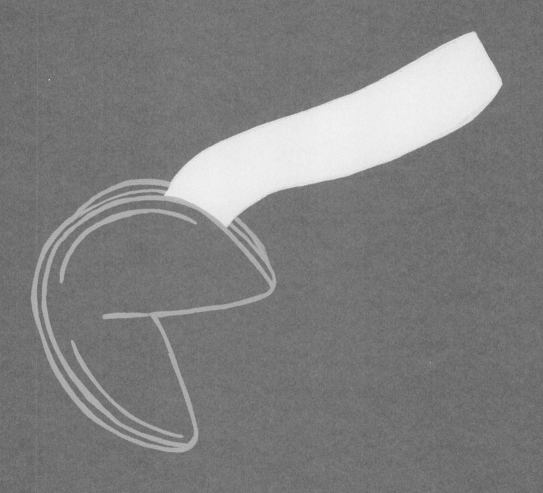

# TRUTH

I'm scared of being a failure at . . .

**DARING**

Sign up to do something you might fail at. Something that doesn't come naturally, something you might be truly terrible doing. And then do it. Plan to fail.

# BUT
# ENJOY
# YOURSELF
# ANYWAY.

**DOUBLE DARING**

Come back to this page after you've finished your most-likely-to-fail activity and describe what happened. Did you actually fail? Or does the fact that you went through with it mean it wasn't a total failure, no matter the actual outcome? Sometimes taking a risk, even if it doesn't end perfectly, gives us a chance to see a situation or ourselves in a new light. With that in mind, if you were to tell someone else about your experience, how would you describe it?

# TRUTH

My style icon is . . .

# DARING

Style is as much about your attitude as it is about *what* you wear, so today, try a new look. Wear your hair a different way. Put your outfit together differently than you normally do. Accessorize with something unexpected. Experiment a little. Maybe you have something you've wanted to wear but have been too self-conscious to try. Rock it! It's exhilarating to get outside your comfort zone, to take a risk every once in a while. If it's too much to even consider wearing your new look all day, just go out for a little bit—you stylish, daring thing, you.

# TRUTH

When did you last feel most confident?

_____

_____

_____

_____

_____

_____

_____

_____

_____

_____

_____

_____

_____

_____

_____

_____

_____

_____

_____

_____

_____

_____

_____

Confidence is a skill, and that means you can build it. Make a list of things that you're good at, things that make you feel confident, and whenever you are feeling nervous or scared or shy, read this list and channel your inner boss.

DOUBLE DARING

The next time someone compliments you, don't be overly modest or humble. Don't disagree or shrug it off. We are taught to act as if we don't care about praise so that we don't seem arrogant, but being proud of something you do well doesn't make you cocky. Own it. Say thank you. You can be gracious *and* proud. And be sure to come back to this list every once in a while and add to it. It will serve as a reminder to recognize yourself, to appreciate what you do well.

# TRUTH

When was the last time you had an adventure?

DARING

Invite some adventure into your life. Close your eyes, point to this page, and then open your eyes. Do the dare your finger is resting on!

**BE 10 MINUTES LATE FOR SOMETHING TOMORROW.**
Play hooky for a bit (even if it's just for a few minutes) and do something out of the ordinary with your extra time.

**GO OUTSIDE AND GET DIRTY!**
Plant a seed.
Sweat a little.

**WALK HOME.**
From anywhere.

**BUILD SOMETHING.**
A sandcastle. A fire. Anything that strikes your fancy!

# TRUTH

What has been your biggest mistake (to date)?

DARING

Rewrite the story of your biggest mistake like a success story. What did you learn from it? Why was it good that you made that mistake in particular? We all make mistakes, no matter who we are, what we do, or where we live. HUMAN = mistake maker.

TRUTH

Who are you jealous of and why? _____

_____

_____

_____

_____

_____

_____

_____

_____

_____

_____

_____

_____

_____

_____

_____

_____

_____

_____

_____

_____

_____

_____

_____

_____

Jealousy is totally normal. Acknowledging it and letting it out gives the feeling less power so you can move on. But can you be happy—really happy—for the person you're jealous of? First, you'll have to find a way to accept the person you are, flaws and all. And then try to accept who *they* are. It's not easy (and probably something you'll spend the rest of your life working on), but learning to be happy for those we love, those we keep in our lives, is essential so that we aren't held back by resentment and negativity. Ultimately, we are the ones who live with our feelings—we can't escape our own thoughts and emotions—and an effort to be generous and happy for someone else will also be a gift to yourself.

# TRUTH

Imagine you're the hero in a comic. What's your superpower?

DARING

Write a short story for the hero version of yourself, or draw the superhero version of yourself. Fleshing out this heroic narrative makes it more real. You are powerful!

"DON'T TELL ME WOMEN ARE NOT the STUFF OF HEROES."

— QIU JIN, 19th century poet, feminist, and REVOLUTIONARY

## TRUTH

When was the last time you unplugged? What were you doing?

# DARING

See if you can go for three hours (when you aren't sleeping!) without looking at your phone.

# DOUBLE DARING

Feeling extra bold? Put your phone away for 24 hours—no checking! You may feel anxious at first, or you may not, but notice how you feel and how often you are tempted to grab your phone or check your computer for any reason.

# SIT WITH THE FEELINGS.

# TRUTH

What labels have other people put on you? What names (good *or* bad) have you been called?

# DARING

Pick a label that actually reflects how you see yourself. Something you're good at or a quality that makes you special. Something you want to be known for. Write it down and tape it up next to your bed. Look at the word first thing in the morning and right before you go to sleep at night.

# DOUBLE DARING

## MAKE A REAL LABEL FOR YOURSELF.

Cut out a piece of paper with your label written on it and tape it to your shirt or bag. Maybe it's a positive word—something you rock—or maybe you're taking a negative label, a word other people have called you, and turning it on its head. Wear your label around for a day. What kind of responses do you get? Do people ask you about it? How do you describe it to them?

# TRUTH

What do you wish you could change about the world?

Use your voice! Pick one of the options below and share your passion. Be LOUD and PROUD.

- **Get political:** Send a letter to your senator about something you care about. Put yourself on the record as a passionate citizen.
- **Talk it out:** Talk to a friend about how you really feel about something. Only one rule—no apologizing (unless you've actually done something wrong).
- **Be a human billboard:** Make a sign about an issue you care about and wear it around today.

"NONE OF US CAN KNOW WHAT WE ARE CAPABLE OF UNTIL WE ARE Tested."

—DR. ELIZABETH BLACKWELL, the first woman in the United States to graduate from medical school

# TRUTH

How do you deal with stress? What causes you the most stress?

Stand up. Slowly lift your arms out and away from your body in a sweeping motion toward the sky. When your hands are directly above your shoulders, look up. Take deep breaths in and out. Do your hands feel heavy above your head? What are your legs and feet doing? How does the air feel when it fills your lungs? It's so easy to get caught up in the minutiae of our day-to-day, to be harried by all the things that have to get done, that sometimes we miss the fact that this is life. This is it. Taking a minute to breathe can reconnect you with the moment, with the life you are living.

# TRUTH

Being alone makes me feel . . . _____

_____

_____

_____

_____

_____

_____

_____

_____

_____

_____

_____

_____

_____

_____

_____

_____

_____

_____

# OWN YOUR ALONE TIME.

Next Friday night, make a date with yourself. Go to dinner (yes, and sit there alone), go see a movie, or just curl up and read a book if that makes you happy. But make a plan for the night. Even if you're later invited to do something else, consider yourself booked, because you already have plans—with yourself. And there's no better company! At the end of the night, note what came up for you. Did you feel moments of loneliness or worry that you were missing out on something? Or was it a relief to be able to do exactly what you wanted to, without having to worry about anyone else? Sometimes we get overbooked and forget to schedule real quality alone time for ourselves.

# TRUTH

If I could take back one thing I've said to someone I love, it would be . . .

**DARING**

Call someone. Not just anyone, but someone you've been thinking about but haven't had the guts to call, maybe lately or maybe ever. No texting—you have to call. And if there's no answer, you have to leave a message.

# TRUTH

Have you ever trusted someone with a secret that they didn't keep? Have you ever betrayed someone else's secret?

Confess your deepest, darkest secret. Write it down here. And then take a thick, black marker and scribble over it. Black out every single word. Now your confession exists, but it's hidden from everyone except you. It can stay here until you are ready to share it.

DOUBLE DARING

Be open to the idea that you might want to share your secret with someone you trust. Sometimes when we let things go, they lose their power over us. Just be sure you share your secrets with people who really care about you—people who have your best intentions at heart.

TRUTH

Have you ever had a confrontation with a stranger? What happened?

DARING

Do something kind for yourself. Reach around and rub your own shoulders.
Close your eyes and think about your favorite vacation spot. Do you feel
kinder after you've given yourself a little love?

# TRUTH

What makes you really, really mad?

DARING

# FEEL THE RAGE.

Let it out. Scream at the top of your lungs. Write a list of things you hate. Anger is *not* bad. It can be motivating—and a powerful tool to change a situation that's not working for you. Plus it's usually a secondary emotion, which means it might be masking something else.

## SO LET IT OUT,
## UNLEASH IT,
## AND SEE WHAT'S LEFT.

# TRUTH

Have you ever been talked into something you didn't want to do?

_____
_____
_____
_____
_____
_____
_____
_____
_____
_____
_____
_____
_____
_____
_____
_____
_____
_____
_____
_____
_____
_____
_____
_____
_____
_____
_____
_____
_____

Saying no takes practice, but it's as important as saying yes. So today, just say no. Say no to something you don't want to do but feel like you should. Say no and don't do it, even if you're disappointing someone. Imagine how disappointed you would be in yourself if you couldn't say no when you wanted or needed to.

**ON THE FOLLOWING PAGES** you'll find eight inspiring quotes from women who dared to follow their passions and find their own way. They took risks, they made mistakes, they had major triumphs and huge failures. They are heroes because they didn't let critics or disappointment stop their search for truth. And because of their dogged, daring determination, they found it.

Use the blank space for note-taking and for thoughts and activities as you use this journal. Jot down other quotes from people that inspire you. Or write your own mantras, words that you want to live by—your own inspiring quotes. After all, greatness isn't born. It's grown and nurtured. The great women on the following pages became truly great in the process of finding themselves. And so will you!

Make the most of YOURSELF by fanning the TINY SPARKS OF POSSIBILITY into flames of ACHIEVEMENT.

— GOLDA MEIR, the first female Prime minister of Israel

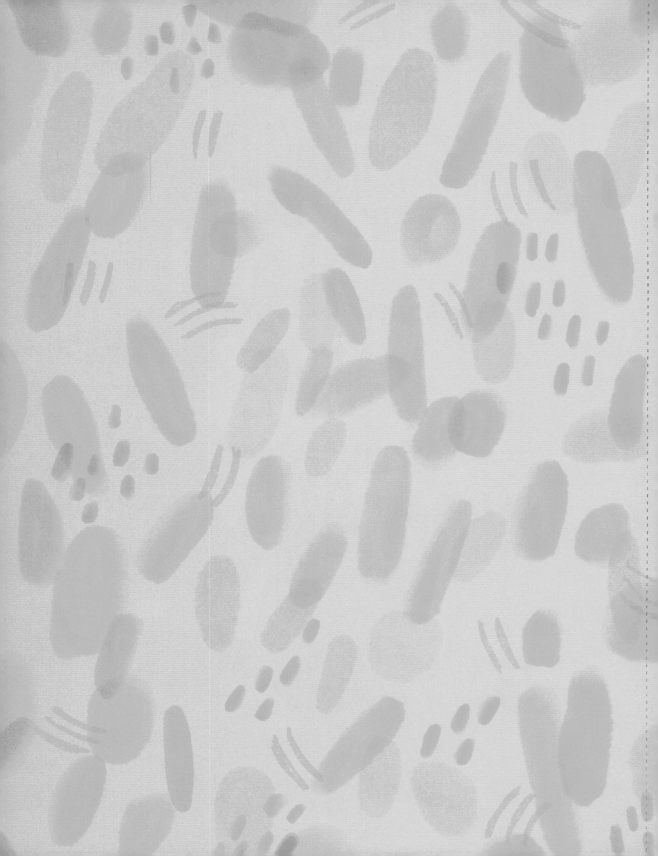

# WHAT I AM LOOKING FOR IS NOT OUT THERE, It is in ME.

— HELEN KELLER, author, activist, humanitarian, and the first deaf-blind person to earn a bachelor of arts degree

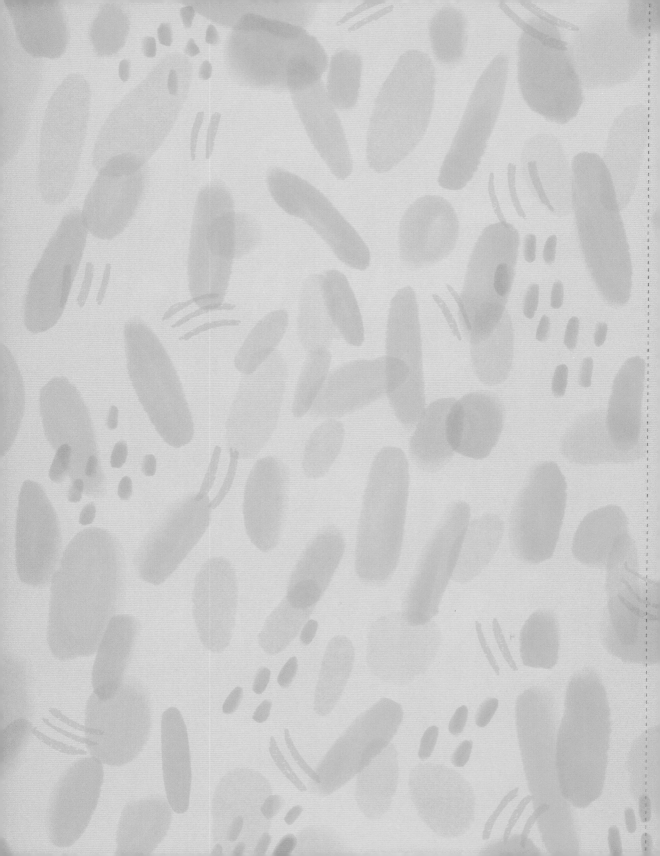

# I AM NOT AFRAID OF STORMS FOR I AM LEARNING HOW TO SAIL MY SHIP.

-LOUISA MAY ALCOTT,
abolitionist, feminist, novelist, and the author of Little Women

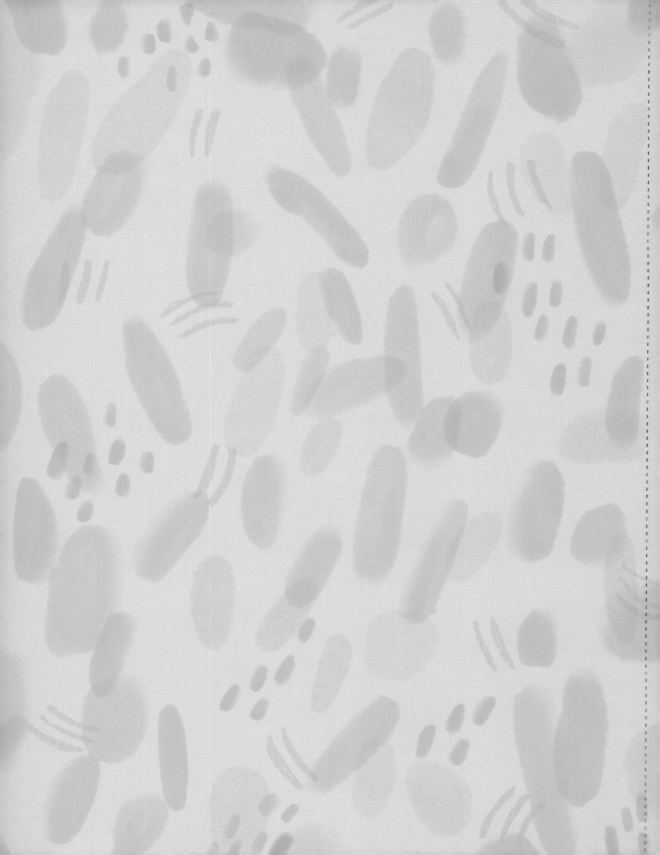

TRUTH is so RARE that it is DELIGHTFUL to TELL it.

—EMILY DICKINSON, one of the greatest American poets

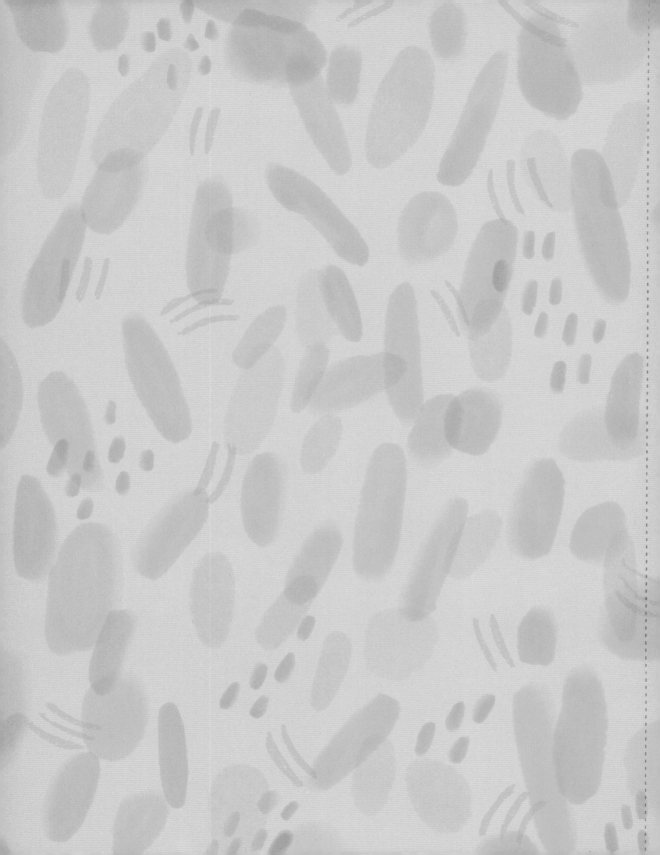

We MUST HAVE PERSEVERANCE and ABOVE ALL CONFIDENCE in ourselves.

—MARIE CURIE, pioneering physicist and chemist, the first woman to win a Nobel PRIZE, and the first person to win two Nobel Prizes

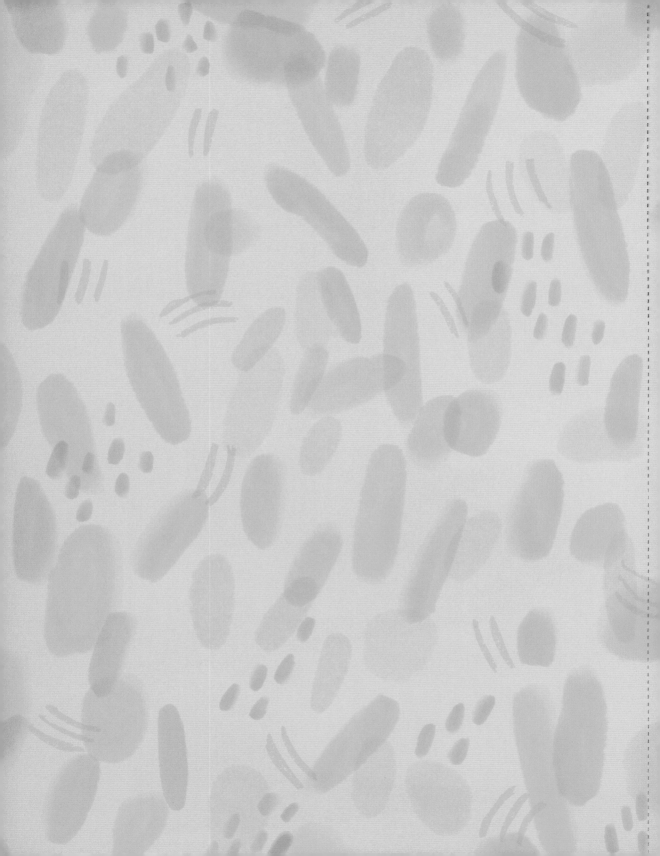

I ENDEAVOR TO MAKE the MOST OF EVERYTHING.

—VICTORIA WOODHULL, the first woman to be nominated and to campaign for the United States presidency

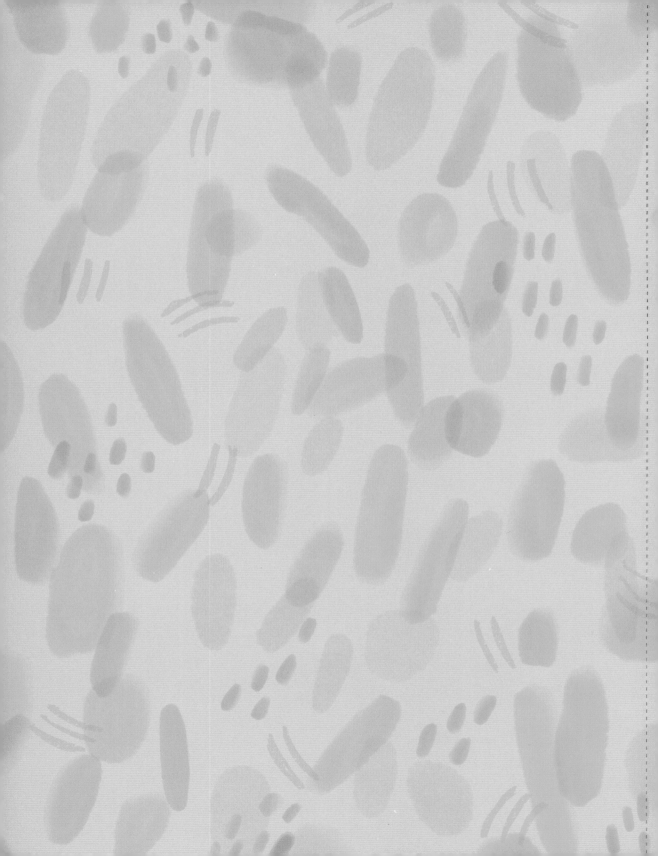

IMAGINATION is the only key to the FUTURE. Without it none exists— WITH IT ALL THINGS are POSSIBLE.

—IDA TARBELL, author and journalist, and one of the leading "muckrakers" of the late 19th Century

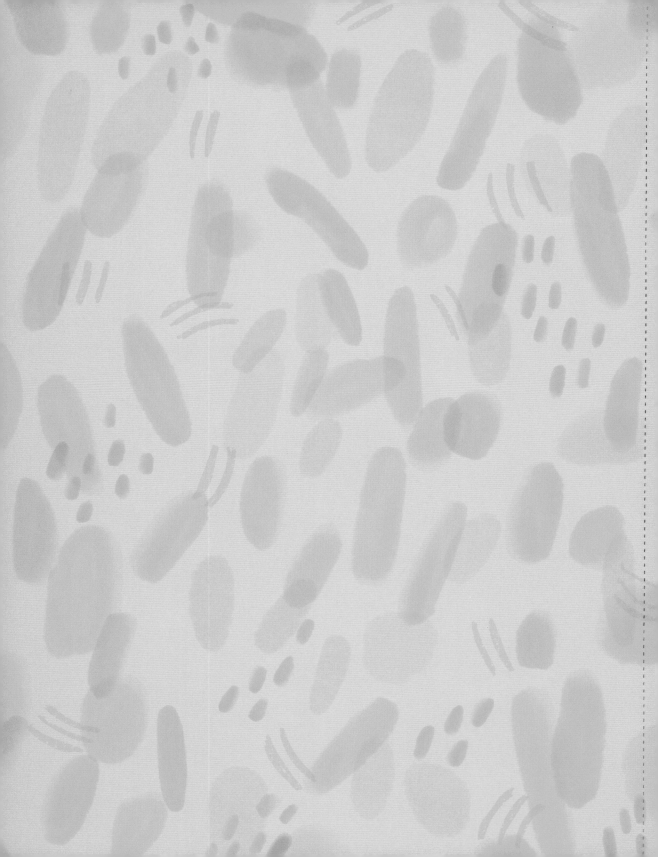

# FAILURE IS IMPOSSIBLE.

— SUSAN B. ANTHONY,
women's rights activist and suffragist
who played a pivotal role in women
getting the right to vote

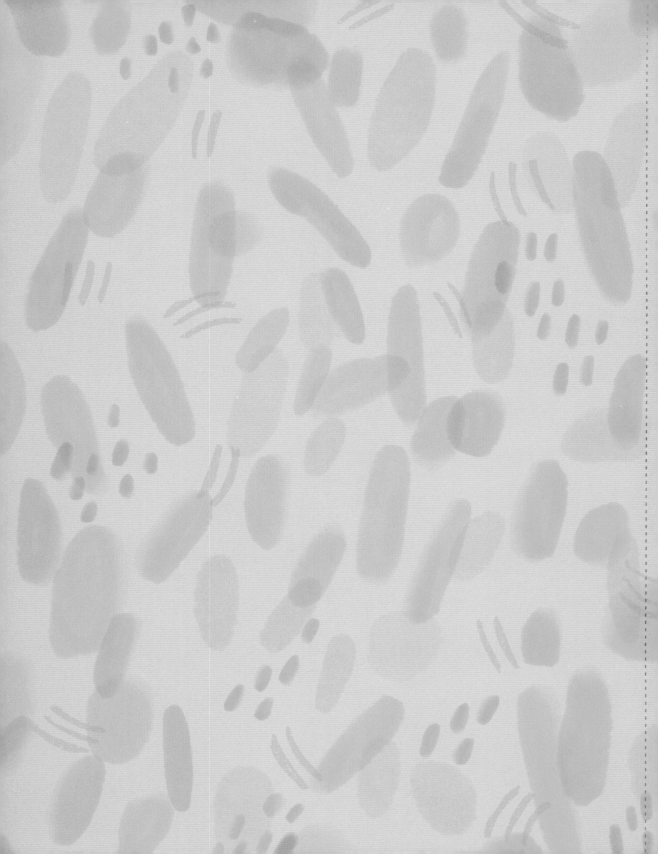

I REFUSE to take no for an ANSWER.

—BESSIE COLEMAN, aviator, and the first woman of African American or Native American descent to hold a pilot's license

# TRUTH

When was the last time you asked for something you wanted? What did you ask for? Did you get it?

**DARING**

Asking for what you want takes practice. Write a script for yourself—a guide that outlines how you would ask for something—and imagine actually asking. Imagine yourself in front of your boss, a friend, or a family member. Plan out what you'll say and envision how you'll feel if you get it.

**DOUBLE DARING**

# ASK!

Take the script you wrote, and the next time you're wavering on whether or not to go for something, put it to good use. What's the worst thing that could happen? Someone says no and you're in the same position you are now? But what if they say yes and you get what you want? Stop putting it off and go for it!

# TRUTH

Do you have a friend you've drifted apart from, or a friendship that isn't what it used to be?

Think about someone you wish you were in better touch with, and reach out. You have to be brave to take the first step, but friendship takes work and effort. Don't be afraid to be the person who initiates. After all, if you end up rekindling or strengthening a friendship, it will be largely in thanks to your willingness to make it happen! If it doesn't end up going anywhere, you really haven't lost anything—and now you'll know you tried.

"FAR AWAY in the SUNSHINE ARE MY HIGHEST ASPIRATIONS. I MAY NOT REACH THEM, BUT I CAN LOOK UP AND SEE THEIR BEAUTY, BELIEVE IN THEM, AND TRY TO FOLLOW WHERE THEY Lead."

— LOUISA MAY ALCOTT, abolitionist, feminist, novelist, and the author of Little Women

# TRUTH

What do you do for show? Is there something you find yourself doing or posting about just because you want people to see you doing it, not because it's necessarily important to you or even something you *want* to do?

DARING

## RESIST THE URGE TO COMMENT.

Can you go a day without commenting or liking anything online? What about a week? Does liking things or commenting change the things you do (and post) for show?

# TRUTH

Is the voice in your head too harsh sometimes? What are the stories you tell yourself that you wish you could change?

DARING

Write down an alternate story, a kinder message for yourself, fold it up, and put it in your pocket. Carry it around today and pull it out when you feel yourself getting frustrated or overwhelmed, and read your new story. Treat yourself like you would treat a friend or a loved one.

"I HONOR EVERY WOMAN WHO has STRENGTH ENOUGH TO STEP out of the BEATEN PATH WHEN SHE FEELS THAT HER WALK LIES IN ANOTHER."

— HARRIET HOSMER, considered to be the first female professional sculptor

# TRUTH

What do you wish people would notice about you?

DARING

Compliment someone you know on something that has nothing to do with how they look. Stick to things they've done or personality traits they have. Go deep and be sincere. How do they react?

# TRUTH

We live in a world that's very focused on self-improvement. We are often told that practice makes perfect, and we are surrounded by metrics by which to measure our accomplishments. What's something you've felt pressure to improve about yourself?

DARING

What would happen if you stopped striving toward perfection just for one day? What if you just went about your life not trying to be better or bigger or faster at something? Try it. What happens when you try to do things "well enough" and not "perfectly"?

**TRUTH**

How much time do you spend thinking about how you look?

# DARING

Get ready without a mirror and then go out without checking to see how you look. Come back and write how it felt. When you were out, did you think about your looks more or less?

# DOUBLE DARING

Go the entire day without looking at yourself. Was it liberating or anxiety-inducing not to know if you had something stuck in your teeth or what your hair looked like? Did you care more or less?

# TRUTH

Is nature important in your life? What does it mean to you?

**DARING**

Set your alarm early tomorrow and watch the sun rise. There's power in the natural world, a wild awe that can come from witnessing something so much bigger than we are. Notice what the sky looks like, how the colors of the objects around you change as the sun changes position. What do you find yourself thinking about? Do you feel closer to nature, closer to the world around you?

# TRUTH

What habit do you wish you could break?

What habit do you wish you could make?

It's been said that it takes 21 days to break a habit and 2 months to make a new habit stick, but it all starts with one simple decision. Once you've made a choice to do something, you've taken the first step. Think about a habit you want to build or something you're trying to stop. Maybe you want to become a better writer, or maybe you want to stop biting your nails or always running late. Make a decision to make or break a habit, and write your goal down here. What are the reasons you have for wanting to do this? Write them all down (whether it's one or ten reasons!), and come back and read this list once a day for the next week to remind yourself of your choice and why you want it. The reminder will help you on your way.

# TRUTH

Would you rather have too much money or too much time?

DARING

Take a mental-health day. Let yourself take a day off, a day away from responsibility and to-do lists, and all the things you *should* be doing. Spend the day doing something for pure enjoyment. What brings you joy?

# TRUTH

If money didn't matter, what is the one thing you would buy for yourself?

# LIFE IS ABOUT EXPERIENCES.

The next time you have a few extra dollars, don't buy anything with it. Instead, set the money aside for an actual experience. Go see a movie. Go visit a local museum or gallery (and use the cash to get there by bus, or use it for the entry fee). How does it feel to spend your money on a moment instead of an object? Does it last longer? How long does it stay with you?

# TRUTH

Think about the last time you were really inspired. What happened? What did it feel like?

Today, give inspiration a chance to strike by mixing things up a bit. Do something different, and maybe you'll feel something different. Inspiration can come from the strangest places and can strike at truly unexpected moments! Try one of these:

- **Change your morning routine.** Get up 15 minutes earlier. Do things out of order.
- **Take a different route to wherever you're going.**
- **Stand up and do 11 jumping jacks.** Yes, right now.

List some other things you would like to try:

# TRUTH

If a friend were to fill out this form about you, what would they say? Would it differ from how you would describe yourself? Fill in both and compare. Don't worry if they're different—it makes sense that they would be. After all, no one could possibly know you as well as you know yourself.

## YOU DESCRIBING YOU

The person I most admire:

When I have an hour to myself, I like to:

My most embarrassing moment ever:

I can always be counted on to:

In an emergency, I react by:

Introvert / extrovert / a little of both (circle one)

Nothing makes me happier than:

I would like to be known for being:

If I were going to be famous for anything, it would be:

## HOW A FRIEND WOULD DESCRIBE YOU

Most admires this person:

Would spend an hour alone doing:

Most embarrassing moment ever:

Can always be counted on to:

In an emergency, reacts by:

Introvert / extrovert / a little of both (circle one)

Is happiest when:

Would like to be known for being:

Is most likely to be famous for:

DARING

Write down 10 to 15 words that describe you. Cut each word out and lay them in front of you. Move them around and piece them together to make a poem of you, a poem of who you are. Once you have the poem set, tape the words down here. Or take a picture of the poem so you can keep the words free to move around tomorrow. And move around again the next day. Let the poem of you change with your moods.

# TRUTH

Do you believe in a God or a higher power? Do you have a set of values that you live by?

DARING

Talk to a friend or a family member who has different religious or spiritual beliefs than you about what they believe and why. Learning about what brings meaning into someone's life ultimately brings meaning into your own. It can open your mind, or even just allow you to see someone you care about in a new light. What did you learn?

# TRUTH

Have you ever done something nice for someone totally anonymously? How
did it make you feel?

**CHANGES COME FROM small ACTIONS.**

Today, do something small to change the world, to make one person's life better. Need a few ideas? Try one of these . . .

- **Clear out your cupboards** and take some food to your local food bank.
- **Clean your closet** and take the things you don't need or don't wear or that don't fit you, and donate them to a shelter.
- **Send a card** expressing gratitude to someone who means something to you—a grandparent, a mentor, your local barista, etc.

# TRUTH

What's the hardest, most satisfying physical thing you've ever done?

Go find a mirror and say these words while looking at yourself.

# I AM STRONG.
# I AM STRONG.
# I AM STRONG.

Come back and say this whenever you need a reminder that you are power-ful, you are brave, you are **strong**.

# TRUTH

What's the most impressive thing you've ever created?

# DARING

Make something with your hands today. Build a box out of scrap wood. Braid someone's hair. String beads onto a ribbon and wear it around your neck. Use your hands to actually create something.

# DOUBLE DARING

Tap into your creativity and make something every day for the next week. Maybe you'll find a project that takes a few days to complete, or maybe you'll do something different every single day. Keep notes on what you're making and how it feels to be producing something simply for the sheer joy of creation.

# TRUTH

Where do you feel most at peace?

## MAKE SPACE FOR YOURSELF.

Literally. Clear a corner or a section of your room of everything except the rug or carpet. Try to make it big enough so you can sit comfortably, or even lie down. Leave it this way for a week and spend a few minutes relaxing in your space every day. Claim it as your own.

# TRUTH

What was the last truly beautiful thing you saw?

Notice the world around you. Go for a walk and write a poem using the words on the street signs you see. Open a magazine or a newspaper and write a short story based on what you read. The next time you go outside, look up before starting on your way. Appreciating beauty around you can enhance almost any moment, any experience. And giving yourself permission to take in something meaningful sends yourself a message that you are worthy of such beauty, that you deserve to witness and be part of the marvels of the world.

"BUT WHY LOOK BACK AT ALL? WHY TURN YOUR EYES to your SHADOW WHEN BY LOOKING UPWARD YOU CAN SEE YOUR RAINBOW in the SAME DIRECTION."

—MARIA MITCHELL, the first female astronomer in the United States and the first American scientist to discover a comet

# TRUTH

Imagine yourself in five years—who are you? What's the most important thing in your life? What do you spend your time doing and thinking about?

Write a letter to your future self, the person you will be in five years. Be specific—what do you want your five-years-older self to remember about your current dreams, your loves, your fears? Put the letter in a place where you know you'll find it in five years, or keep it safely tucked within the pages of this journal.

**Sarah O'Leary Burningham** is the author of *Girl to Girl, Boyology,* and *How To Raise Your Parents*. Still a teenager at heart, she's played Truth or Dare more times than she can count. She lives in the Bay Area with her family. Learn more at www.sarahburningham.com.

**Sarah Walsh** is the illustrator of many books and products, including *Draw Bridge* and *Hats of Faith*. Once she was dared to drink pickle juice . . . and she refused. She lives in Kansas City with her family. Learn more at www.sarahwalshmakesthings.com.

Text copyright © 2019 by Sarah O'Leary Burningham.
Illustrations copyright © 2019 by Sarah Walsh.
All rights reserved. No part of this book may be reproduced in any form without written permission from the publisher.

ISBN: 978-1-4521-7091-6

Manufactured in China.

Design by Alice Seiler.
Typeset in PaperCute, Prensa, and TT Norms.
The illustrations in this book were rendered in gouache and mixed media, and composited digitally.

10 9 8 7 6 5 4 3 2 1

Chronicle books and gifts are available at special quantity discounts to corporations, professional associations, literacy programs, and other organizations. For details and discount information, please contact our premiums department at corporatesales@chroniclebooks.com or at 1-800-759-0190.

Chronicle Books LLC
680 Second Street
San Francisco, California 94107

Chronicle Books—we see things differently.
Become part of our community at www.chroniclekids.com.